Secret To Hair Bow Success

By LearnHowToMakeBows.com to accompany your DVD

Copyright 2012. May not be sold, transferred, or shared. You may print one copy for your own personal use. You may sell any bows you make with these instructions. There is extra space on the left margins of the page so you can use a 3 hole punch and place in a binder.

MATERIALS NEEDED

High temp/High heat glue gun (no need to spend more than $6)

High temp/High heat glue sticks (match size of glue sticks to size of gun!)

Small alligator clips (beauty supply store or some craft stores)

Various sizes of French barrettes (in the jewelry section of craft store)

Needle and any color thread (Upholestry thread is the best)

Buttons or other embellishments (at craft store there are all kinds of cute, fun ones)

Wood dowel rods (at craft store in size 5/16 inch to 3/16 inch, your preference) - Only needed for Korker bows

Small wooden clothes pins (at least 12) - Only needed for Korker bows

Scissors (Nice pair of spring loaded scissors will make it easier on your hands)

Measuring/cutting mat or clear ruler

Lighters (have a few on hand)

Cardboard (you can cut this up to make simple templates!)

Ribbon (see instructions to determine size and types of ribbon needed for each bow)

CRAFT STORES

A.C. Moore - www.acmoore.com 1-888-ACMOORE (1-888-226-6673) *Stores in almost every state.

Hobby Lobby - www.hobbylobby.com *Stores in most states. (Currently Hobby Lobby does not have stores in AK, CA, CT, DC, DE, HI, ID, MA, MD, ME, NH, NJ, NV, OR, PA, RI, VT, WA.)

Jo-Ann Fabric and Craft Store - www.joann.com 1-888-739-4120
*Stores in most states. (Currently Jo-Ann does not have stores in HI, MS, WY.)

Michael's - www.michaels.com 1-800-MICHAELS (1-800-642-4235)
*Stores in almost every state.

Sally Beauty Supply (for hair clips) – www.sallybeauty.com 1-866-234-9442 *Get a "Sally Card" to save money throughout the year on your purchases.

ONLINE STORES

Wholesale ribbon: www.theribbonretreatwholesale.com

Finished bottle caps for bow centers: search www.Etsy.com

Ribbon:
www.nashvillewraps.com
www.reasonableribbon.com
www.hairbowcenter.com
www.theribbonspot.com
www.theribboncarnival.com

TIP: Be sure to check for online coupons on the company website before going to the store to save money on your supplies!

TIP: Also try searching the internet for store coupons that you can print from home. You can find coupons on many sites, such as:
www.CouponCabin.com   www.CouponCraze.com
www.DealCatcher.com   www.RetailMeNot.com

(We are not affiliated with any of these websites. We are only suggesting them since we have used them with success and wanted to pass along money saving tips.)

How to Line a Clip for Your Hair Bows

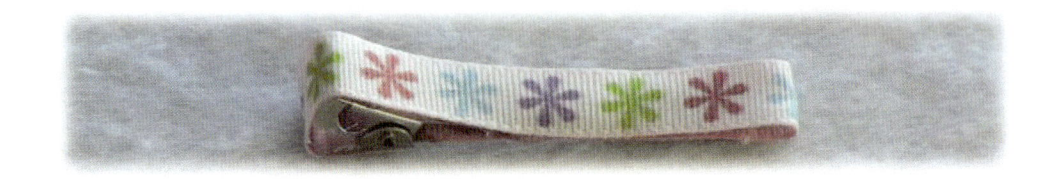

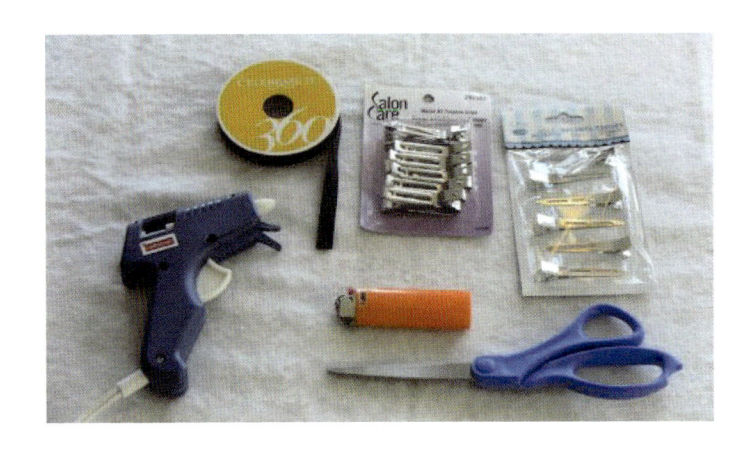

Supplies:
High heat hot glue gun
3/8" ribbon
Clips of your choice (French barrette or alligator clip)
Scissors
Lighter

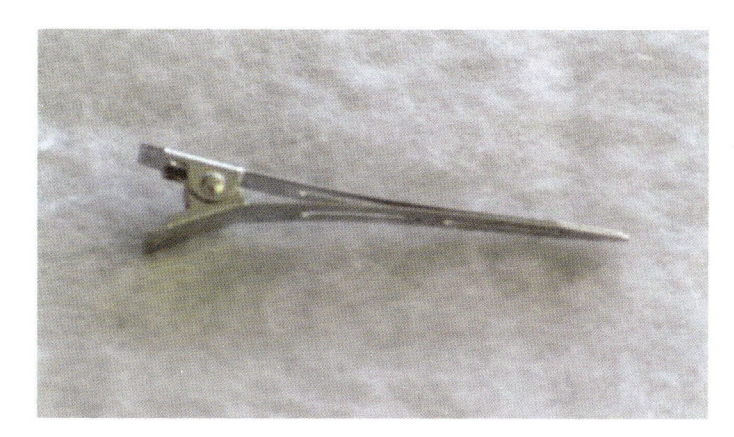

ALLIGATOR CLIP:
Start with the alligator clip like this. The flat side will face up.

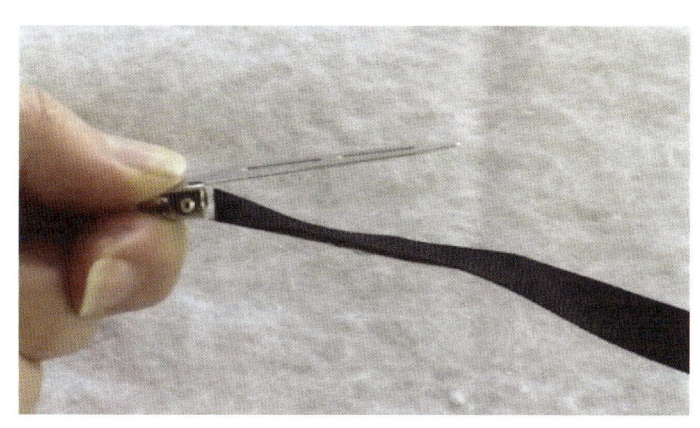

Now open the clip and place the ribbon all the way at the base of the clip as shown and secure with hot glue.

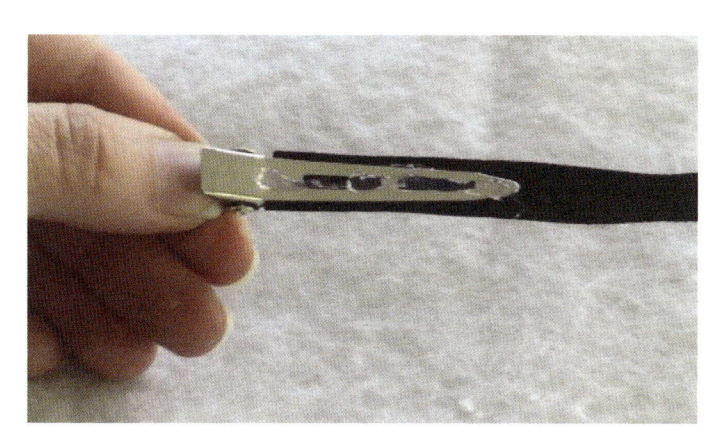

Flip the clip so the bottom is now facing up. Make a line of glue on the clip.

Bring the ribbon around the end of the clip and secure in place.

Copyright 2012.   LearnHowToMakeBows.com   LearnHowToMakeBows@gmail.com

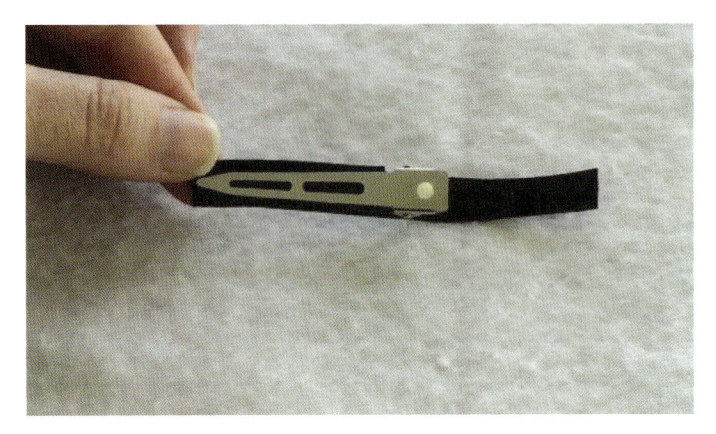

Leave an inch of extra ribbon and cut from the roll.

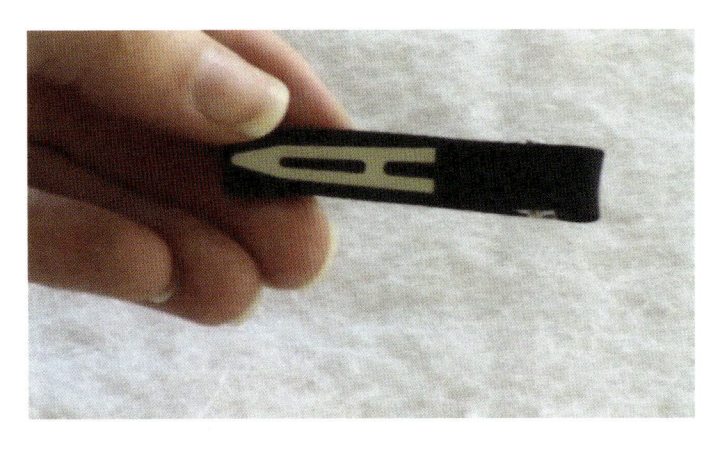

Bring the ribbon around the end of the clip and secure in place with hot glue.

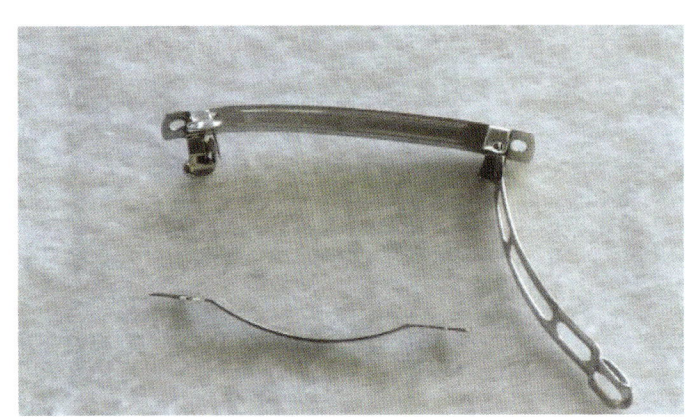

FRENCH BARRETTE: Remove the middle section of the clip as shown. (We'll put it back once the clip is lined.)

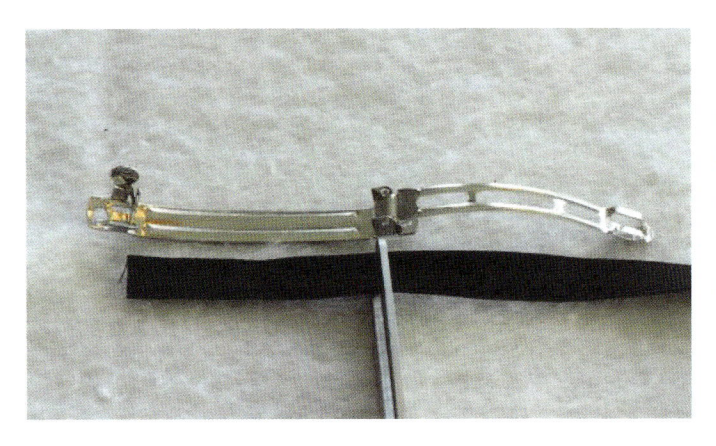

Measure the inside length of the clip and cut a piece of ribbon that exact size. Mine is 2 inches.

Copyright 2012. LearnHowToMakeBows.com LearnHowToMakeBows@gmail.com

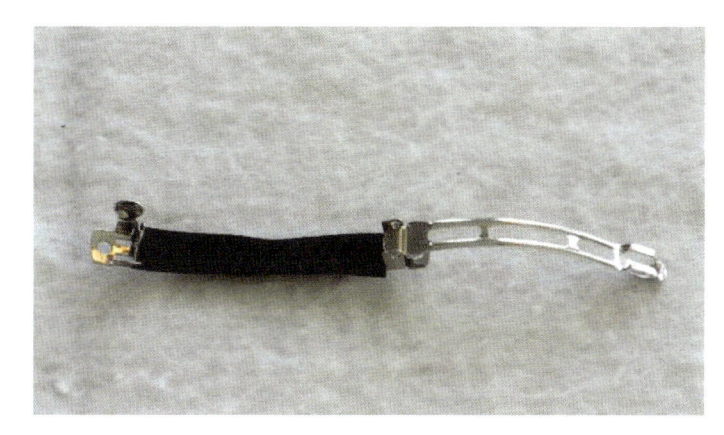

Secure in place with hot glue.

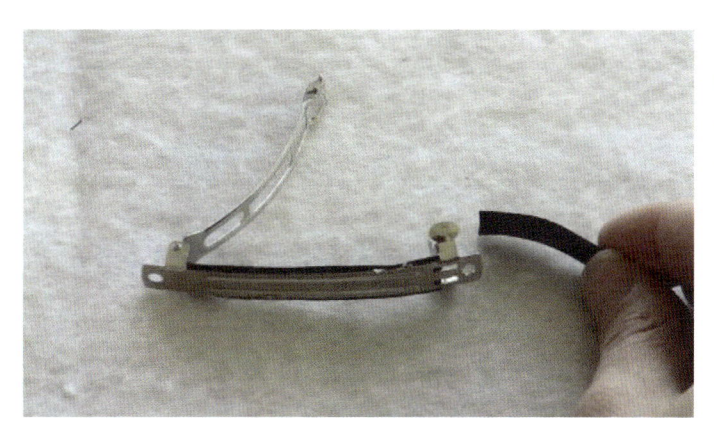

Now flip your clip around and working with the ribbon on the roll start on the open side, as shown.

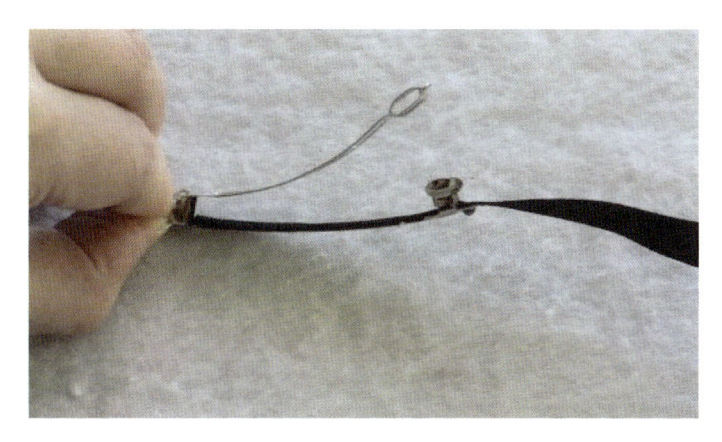

Secure in place on the side facing up. There will just be about ¼ inch of ribbon used.

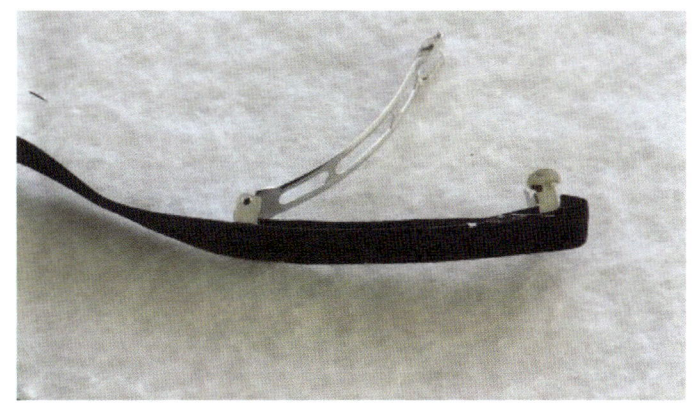

Now bring the ribbon across the clip and secure in place with glue.

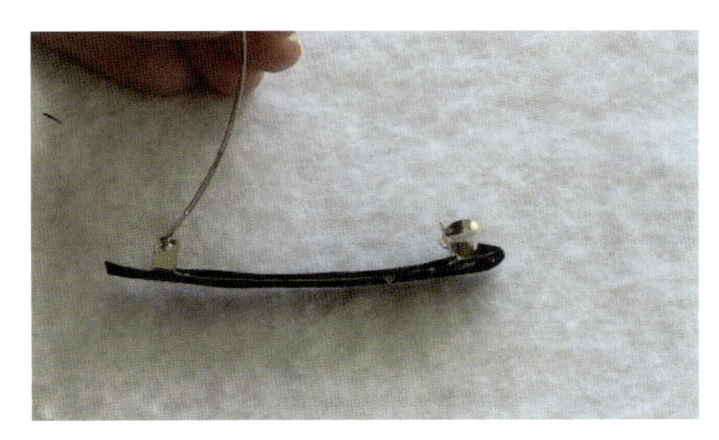

Cut off the extra ribbon leaving just about ¼ inch of ribbon (just enough to wrap around the end.

Trendy Clip

Supplies:
3/8" ribbon
Lined alligator clip
Hot glue gun
Lighter

To start you need a lined alligator clip and an extra piece of ribbon. I'm using a piece that is 1 inch less than 2 times the length of my clip.

Bring the ends of the ribbon together and hot glue in place to form a circle.

Glue the seam side of the circle down to the top of your clip.

Now flip the clip over and open it up. Take a second piece of ribbon and hot glue it down as shown.

Wrap the piece of ribbon around the clip.

When you get the center ribbon to the other side of the clip you'll need to open it up again.

Wrap the center ribbon as shown. Secure in place with glue.

Cut off the excess ribbon; it only needs to cover the width of the clip.

Here is the completed trendy clip.

Flower Bow 1

Supplies:
Ribbon (width of your choice – I prefer 3/8" to 5/8")
Needle and thread
Scissors
Button or gem for the center
Ruler

HELPFUL TIP: Use upholstery thread instead of regular quilting thread since it is much thicker.

Start with 4 pieces of 5 inch long ribbon. I'm using 5/8 inch ribbon. Experiment with different lengths and widths!

One at a time, bring the ends of the ribbon piece together and hot glue to form a circle. Do this with all 4 pieces of ribbon.

Gently fold the circle in half so we can find the center point easily.

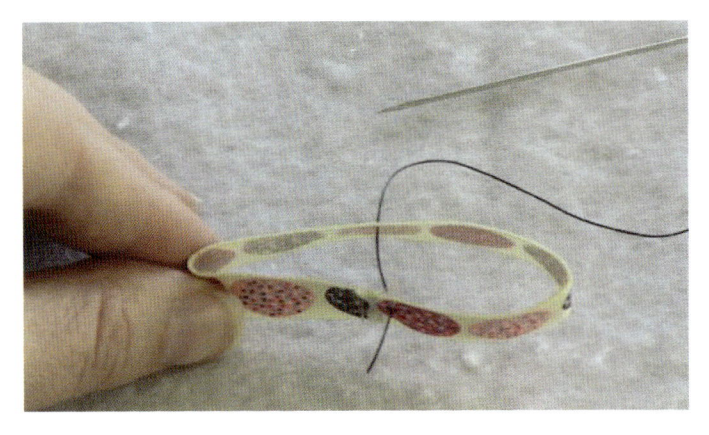

Now you can bring the needle and thread right up through the exact center of your ribbon.

Copyright 2012.   LearnHowToMakeBows.com   LearnHowToMakeBows@gmail.com

Continue to do the same thing with each piece of ribbon and layer them one on top of the other. As you place them on the needle you can fan them out like I've done.

Once you have them all in place and arranged how you like them, bring the needle back through the entire stack of ribbon and secure in place with a stitch.

Now you can glue or sew a button in the center. Hot glue on to an alligator clip and your flower bow is done.

Flower Bow 2

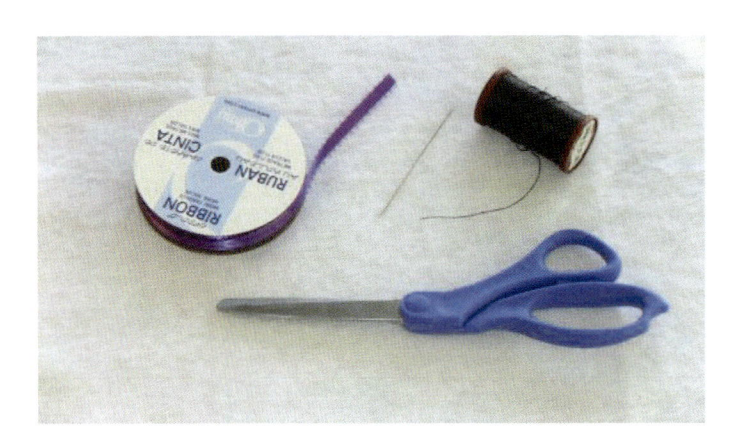

Supplies:
Ribbon (1/4" to 3/8")
Needle and thread
Scissors
Button or gem for the center

IDEA: Try a variety of ribbon widths and number of ribbon pieces used to make all kinds of flowers. You can even use multiple types of ribbon in one bow.

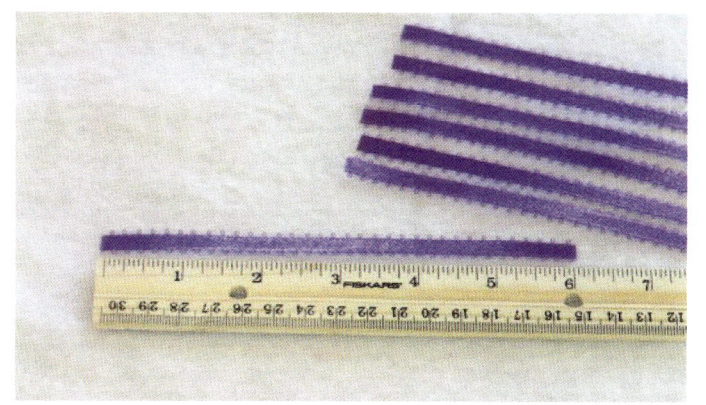

I'm using seven pieces of six inch long ¼" ribbon.

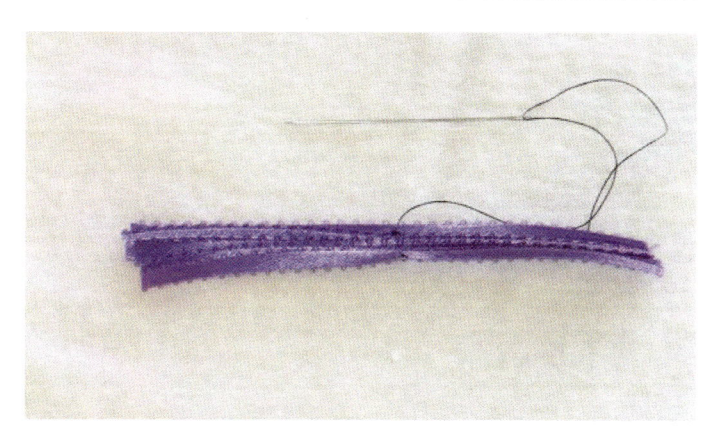

One at a time, place each piece of ribbon on the needle and thread, in the exact center. They will all be stacked on top of each other.

Fan out the ribbons evenly around the center. Hold in place with your finger if you need to so they stay there.

Start with one piece of ribbon and bring it to the center. Poke the needle through the bottom of that ribbon up through the top.

Copyright 2012.   LearnHowToMakeBows.com   LearnHowToMakeBows@gmail.com

Keep going around the circle and do the same thing with each piece so the ends of your ribbon are brought to the center, as shown.

Once they are all in the center, hold it down with your finger and be sure the loops look good.

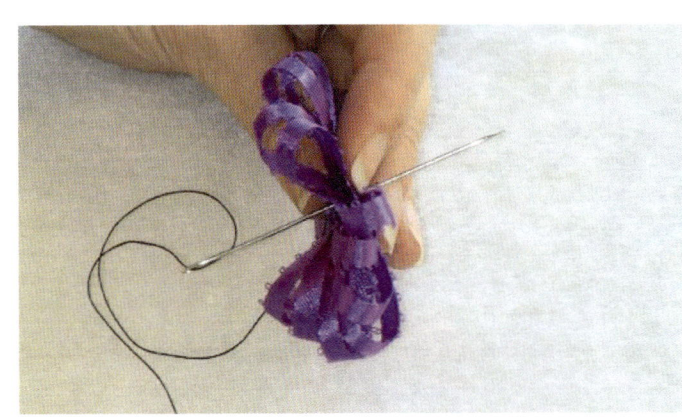

Bring the needle back and forth through the center of the flower at least twice so you can secure the loops in place.

Your flower is now complete. Hot glue it down to the center of a lined alligator clip and glue your choice of button to the center.

Flower Bow 3

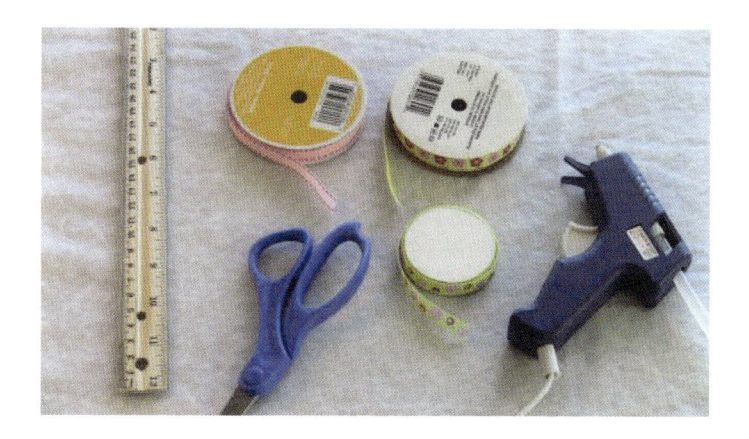

Supplies:
Ruler
3/8" ribbon (3 different colors)
Scissors
Hot glue gun

Cut ribbon strips as follows:
5 pieces 1.25" long
5 pieces 2" long
5 pieces 3" long

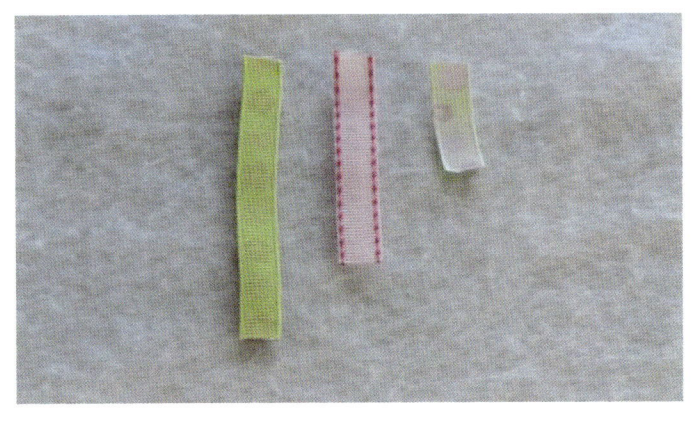

You'll do this 5 times for each petal. First, flip one piece of each length ribbon over so the "bad" side of the ribbon is facing up.

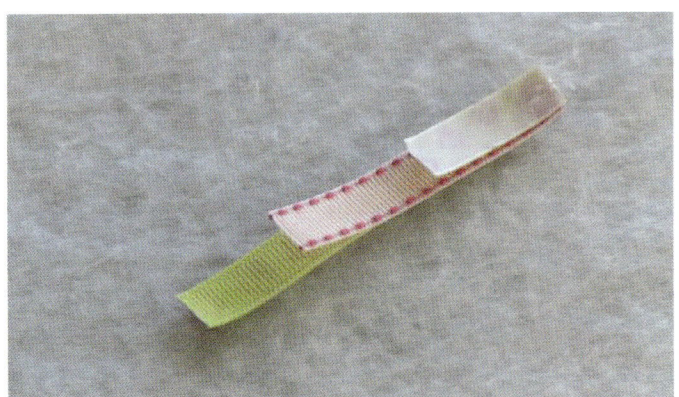

Using a dab of glue in between each layer glue them down from longest up to shortest, as shown. ("Bad" side of ribbon is still facing up.)

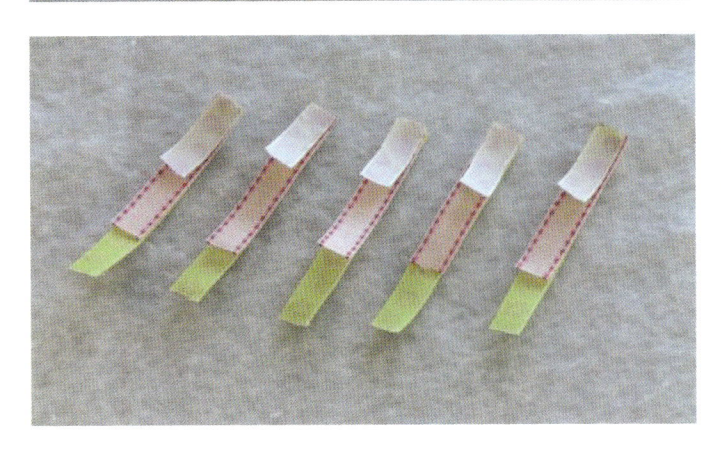

All 5 pieces are complete.

Now bring the ends of the ribbon (starting with the smallest) to the end where you glued the layers down. It will form your petal. You can hold in place with a clip.

Once all pieces are complete you can start gluing them together at the very center, one at a time, in a circle.

Here is the completed flower bow glued down to a lined alligator clip with a button glued down in the center.

Six Loop Bow

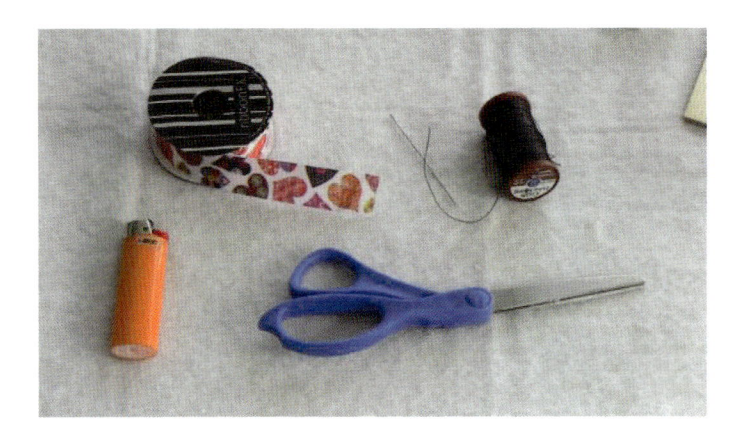

Supplies:
5/8" ribbon (but you can use any width under 1.5")
Needle and thread
Lighter
Scissors
Button for center (if you'd like)
Hot glue gun (for center button)

IDEA: You can even do this same method and make a 4 loop or 8 loop bow!

Working with the ribbon on the roll, loop the end over and secure with a clip (makes it easier!) The size of your loop and size of your tail are determined here!

Now bring the ribbon roll from the top right to the bottom left and make your first loop on the right side.

Bring the ribbon roll to the bottom left to the top right and make your second loop on the left side.

Bring the ribbon roll back to the bottom left to form your second loop on the right side.

Copyright 2012.   LearnHowToMakeBows.com   LearnHowToMakeBows@gmail.com

Repeat this until you have three loops on each side.

(You can stop at 4 loops total or even keep going to get 8 total loops!)

Sew three stitches directly up the center of your bow.

Pull the thread tightly and wrap around the center a few times. Knot the thread at the back of the bow.

Wrap the center with ribbon or glue down a button in the middle. It's now ready to be glued on to a lined clip.

Butterfly Bow

Supplies:
1.5" ribbon
Ruler
Lighter
Scissors
Needle and thread

I'm using 20 inches of 1.5" ribbon.

Make an "awareness ribbon" as shown, with the "bad" side of the ribbon tails facing up.

Bring the tails together and then slide that seam to the center. You'll have the ribbon in a figure 8 shape as shown.
*The skinner the 8, the perkier the bow!

I like to hold the loops at the center and lift them up to be sure they are exactly the same length.

Now bring the end of the loop on the right to the center.

Copyright 2012.   LearnHowToMakeBows.com   LearnHowToMakeBows@gmail.com

Bring the left loop to the center and overlap slightly at that center point. You can check to be sure your loops are all the same size.

Carefully lift the bow and create three nice creases across the center.

Wrap some thread across the center tightly and tie off at the back.

To make the center knot, I'm using 8 inches of ribbon. Loop the tail around to form an "awareness ribbon."

Bring the right tail up and through the center. Pull tightly to form a knot.

Glue the center knot down and wrap the ribbon ends to the back of your bow. Your bow is now complete and ready to be glued to a lined clip.

Pinwheel Bow

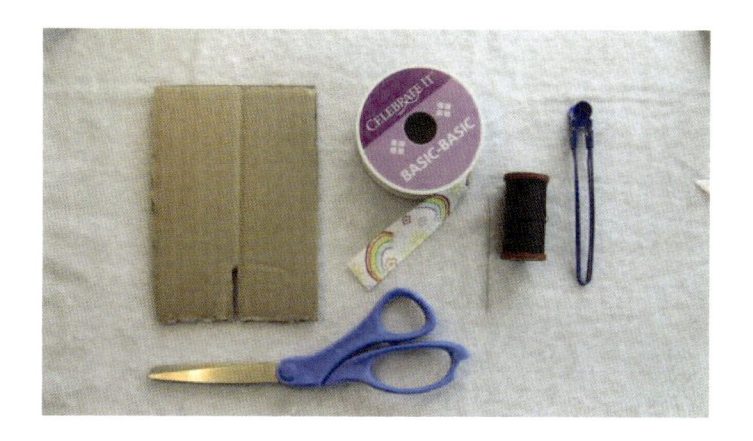

Supplies:
4.5" wide cardboard
Scissors
5/8" ribbon (or your choice)
Needle and thread
Salon clip (from Sally Beauty Supply)

Wrap the ribbon around the 4.5" wide piece of cardboard as shown. The ribbon end is where my thumb is.

You can slide the ribbon off the cardboard and hold in place with a salon clip.

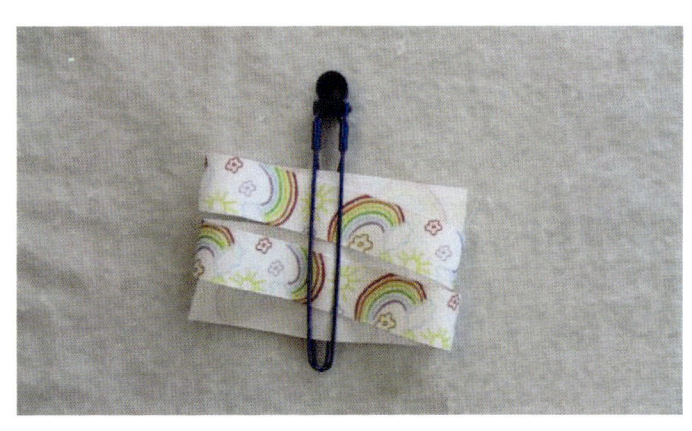

Here's what the back side will look like.

Make 4 stitches directly up the center.

Copyright 2012.   LearnHowToMakeBows.com   LearnHowToMakeBows@gmail.com

Remove the needle and pull the thread tightly. Then wrap it around the center. Your bow will look like this now!

Glue down a button in the center. Your bow is ready to be glued on to a lined clip.

Boutique Bow – 2 Ways!

Supplies:
4.5" wide cardboard
Scissors
1.5" ribbon
Needle and thread
Ruler
Salon clip
Alligator clip

TIP: There are 2 different ways to make a basic boutique bow. I'll show you both. They look a bit different when finished, but are basically the same. Choose to use the method you like the best, but test them both out.

Using the cardboard, wrap your ribbon around it as shown. You can use the ribbon on the roll to make it easier.

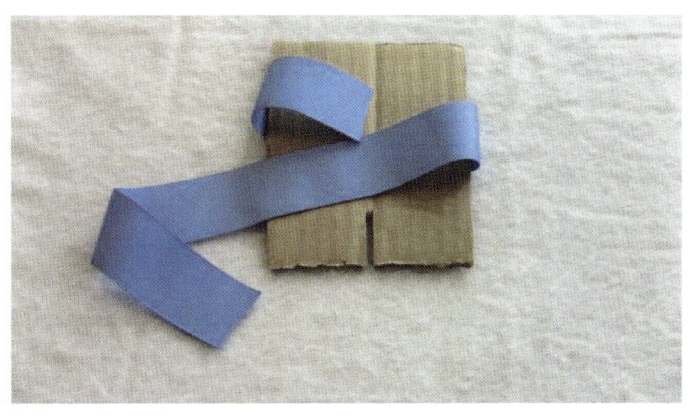

Bring the long tail of the ribbon across and down to the left.

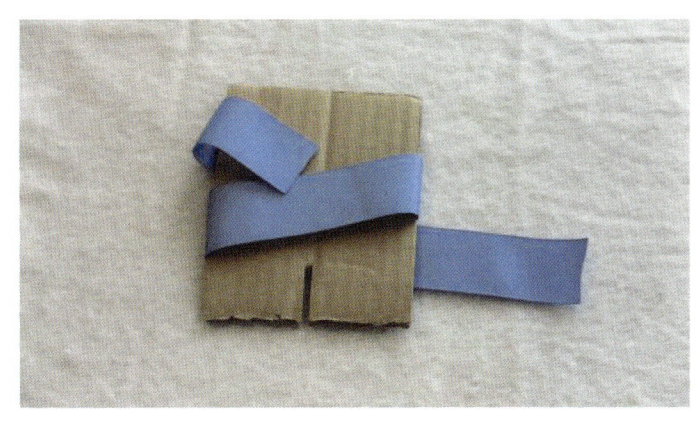

Now bring the tail around the back of the cardboard and to the right.

Finally bring the tail on the right up and to the center. Use a clip to hold in place (makes it easier!)

Here's the back view. Be sure your ribbons are parallel, as shown.

Slide the ribbon gently off the cardboard and hold in place with a salon clip.

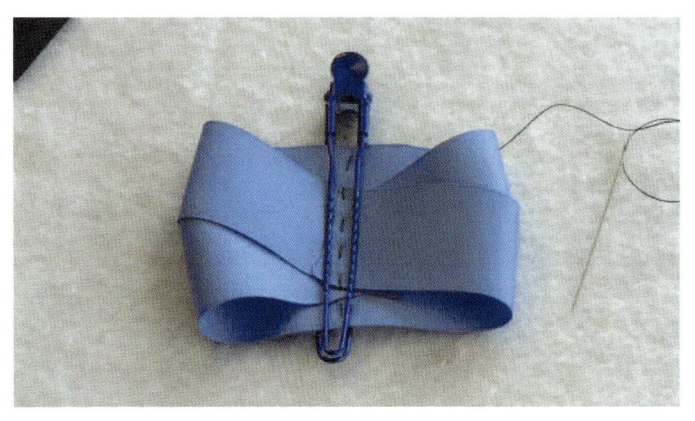

Make 6 stitches directly up the center. (You can also try just 3 stitches, I just like the way 6 stitches makes the center of the bow look.)

Remove the needle and pull the thread tightly to form peaks in the center of your bow.

Copyright 2012.   LearnHowToMakeBows.com   LearnHowToMakeBows@gmail.com

Wrap the thread around the center tightly then bring the needle to the back and insert through the loops of thread to knot in place.

Here is your completed boutique bow. This can be used in any layered bows you want to make or can be used as is and glued to a lined clip.

Here is the second type of boutique bow I'll show you now.

Supplies:
1.5" ribbon
Alligator clip
Salon clip
Lighter
Needle and thread
Ruler

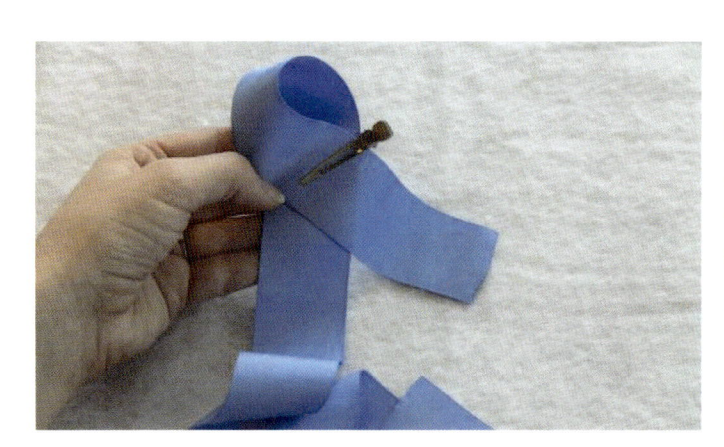

Leaving about a 2 inch tail, loop the ribbon end over and hold in place with a clip.

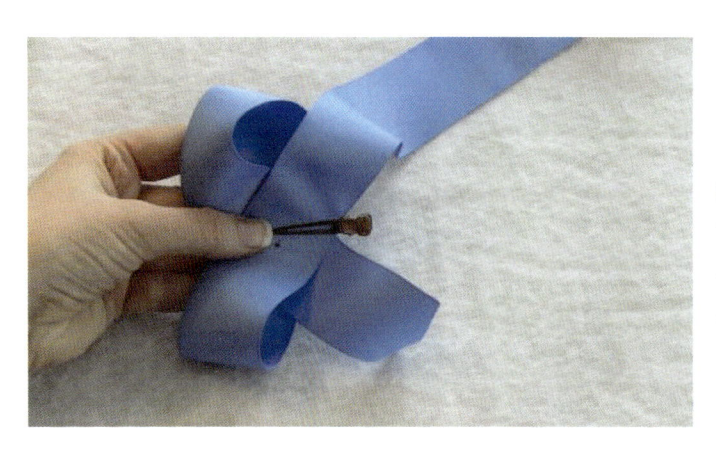

Bring the longer ribbon tail up from the bottom left, across the center and to the top right.

Copyright 2012. LearnHowToMakeBows.com   LearnHowToMakeBows@gmail.com

Bring that end of the ribbon straight down the back of the bow.

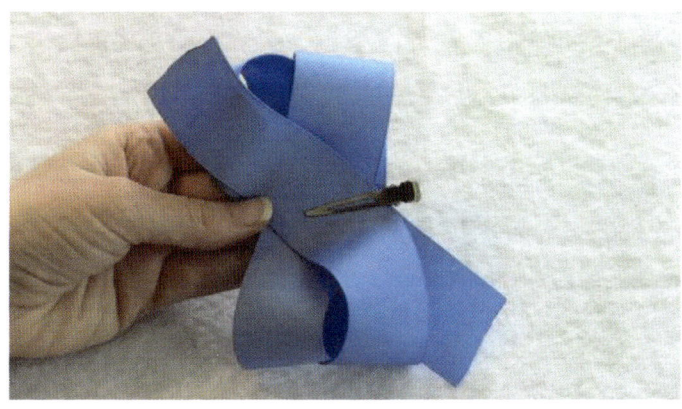

Finally bring that end back up and across your bow to the left side.

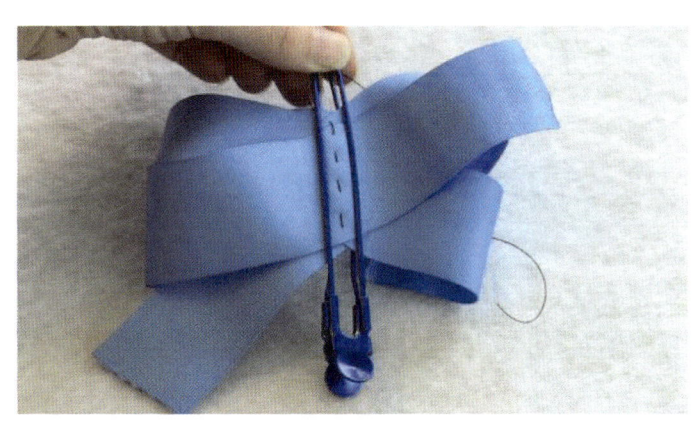

Hold the center in place with a salon clip then stitch up the center. I've made 4 stitches.

Remove the needle and pull the thread tightly so nice peaks form in the center.

Wrap the extra thread around the center a few times and tie off at the back. Your bow is complete.

Heart Ribbon (perfect on a clip!)

Supplies:
Hot glue gun
Lighter
3/8" ribbon (2 pieces 5 inches long, 2 pieces 5.5 inches long)
Scissors

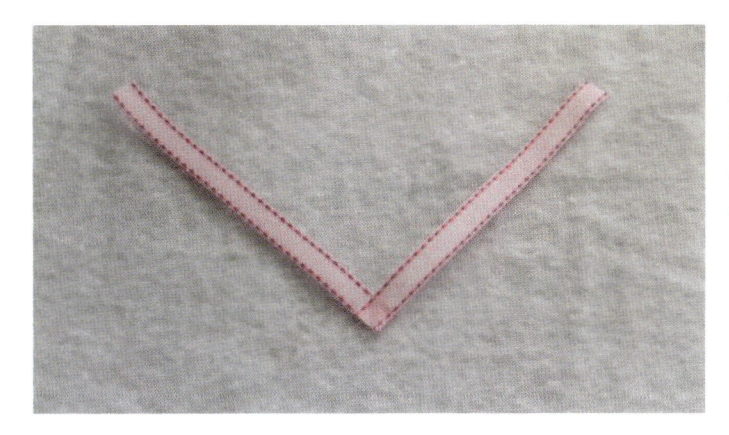

Start with the 2 pieces of 5.5" ribbon and glue down at a 90 degree angle.

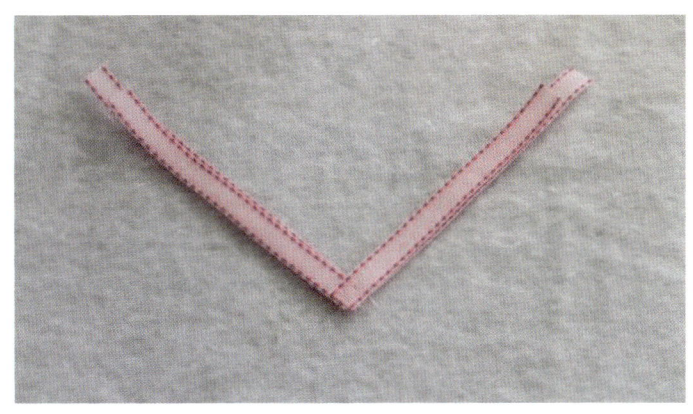

Add the 5" pieces of ribbon directly on top of the 5.5" pieces and glue down at a 90 degree angle in the same way.

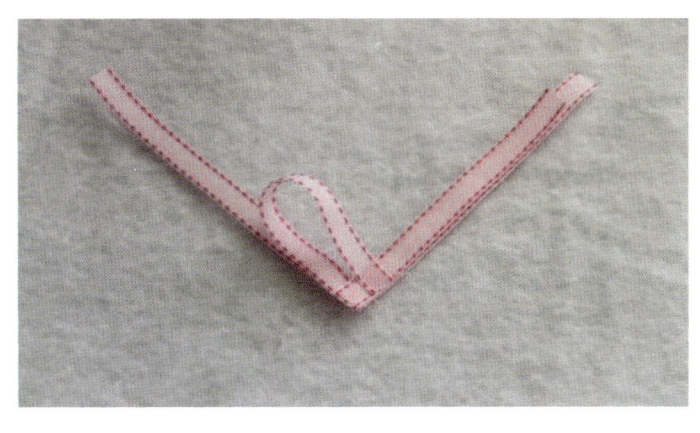

Bring the 5" ribbon end on the left to the corner and glue it down parallel to the 5.5" ribbon on the left.

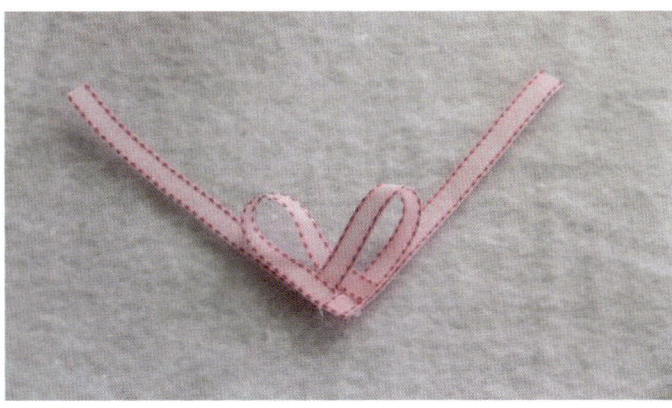

Now bring the 5" ribbon end on the right over the first piece of ribbon it comes across and then under the next piece. Glue down on a 90 degree angle to the 5.5" ribbon on the left.

Bring the 5.5" ribbon from the left to the right and over the first ribbon it crosses, then under the second ribbon. Glue down at a 90 degree angle to the 5.5" right ribbon (and parallel to the 5" ribbon on the left).

Finally bring the 5.5" ribbon on the right over the first piece of ribbon, under the second, and over the third. It should look just like the photo.

Korker Bow

Supplies:
¼" wood dowels
Wood clothespins
3/8" grosgrain ribbon (this works best!)
Lighter
Needle and thread
Ruler
Scissors

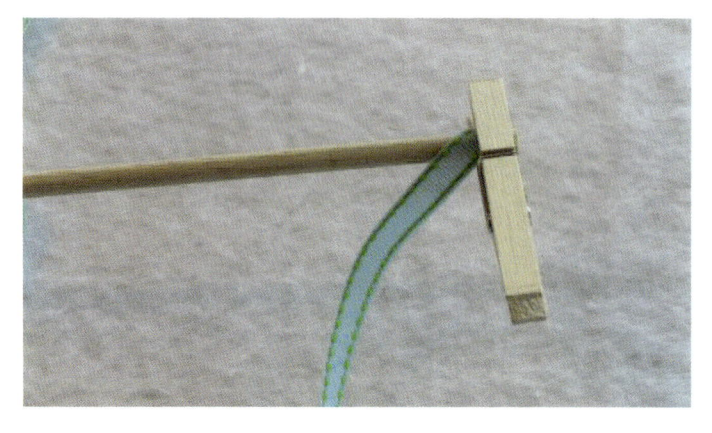

Working with your ribbon on the roll, clip the end at an angle using a clothespin.

Wrap the ribbon at an angle and completely cover the dowel. Don't let the ribbon overlap or separate as you wrap. You shouldn't be able to see any wood.

Place in an oven for 10-15 minutes at 275 degrees. Do not place dark color ribbon next to light colored ribbon; it will bleed.

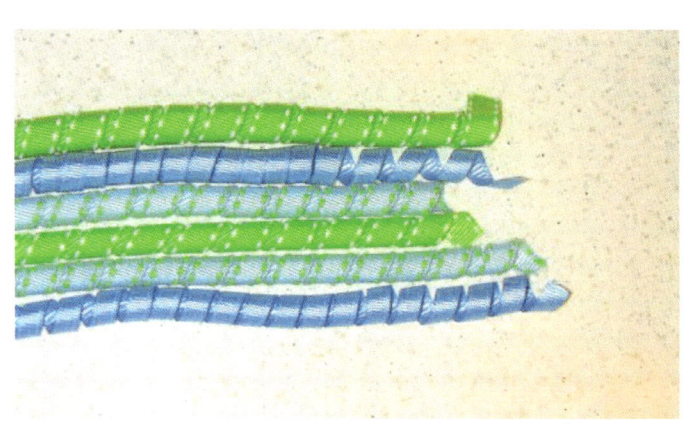

Once it cools for a few minutes, carefully slide off the dowels and you'll have korked ribbon like this!

Cut the ribbon into 2.5" strips. (Or whatever size you prefer.) Then take one at a time and poke the center through your needle/thread.

Continue to place the centers of each piece of ribbon on your needle and thread. I use about 25-30 pieces for a really full and fluffy bow.

Once all the ribbons are on the thread, plus them all tightly together in the center.

Now bring your needle through to the other side of the bow, right at the center. This is going to make sure the thread holds all the ribbon tightly together.

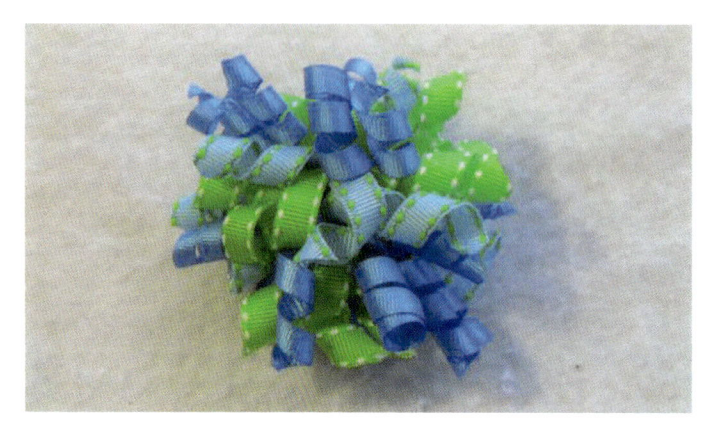

Knot off the thread and your korker bow is now complete. If you make smaller korkers, these are great for the center of your layered bows.

Loops Bow

Supplies:
Scissors
5/8" ribbon
Needle and thread
Ruler

For a small sized bow, I'm using 2.5 inch long strips. Try different lengths for other bow sizes.

I have three different types of ribbon and about 30-40 pieces total.

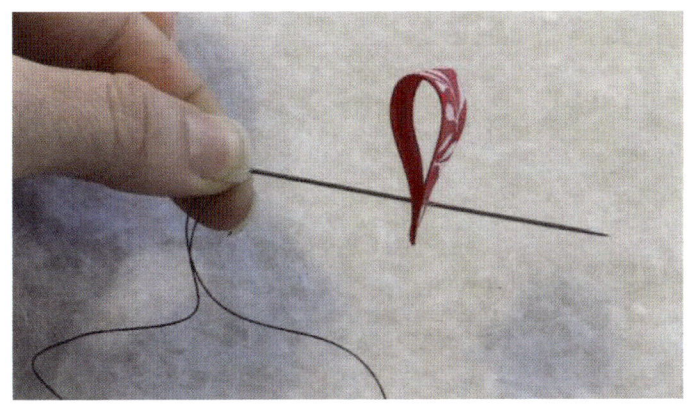

One at a time, loop the ends of a piece of ribbon together ("good" side of the ribbon facing out) and insert the needle/thread about ¼" from the end of the loop.

Continue to place all the ribbon strip loops on the thread. Try to keep all the ends of the ribbons at the bottom.

Now bring the needle through the very first loop you placed on the thread. This will help hold all the loops together tightly.

Fluff out the loops and then you can hot glue the bottom (where you can see the thread) to a lined clip.

Loopy Bow

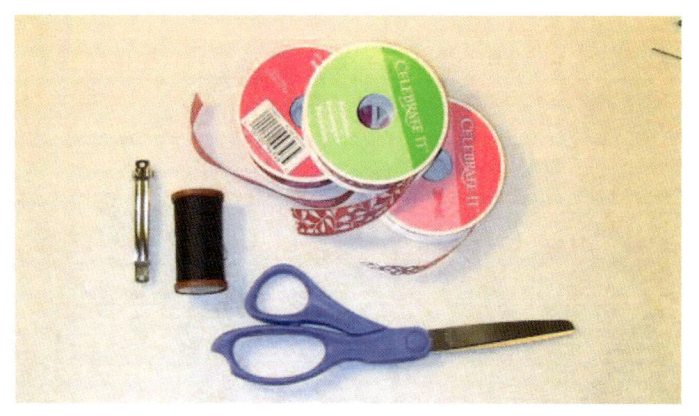

Supplies:
A variety of ribbon widths, colors, patterns (your choice)
Scissors
Thread (upholstery thread is necessary!)
French barrette
Hot glue

Working with your ribbon on the roll, layer the ribbons one on top of the other and hold together with a clip, if you'd like.

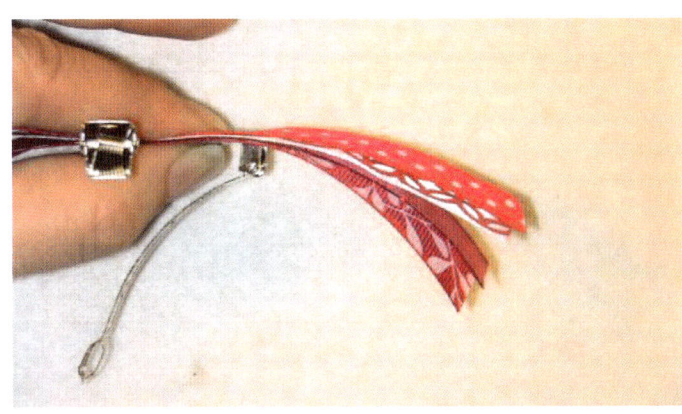

Pop the center piece out of the barrette (like we did when lining these clips). Hold the end of the ribbons on the edge of the barrette and leave an inch or two for tails.

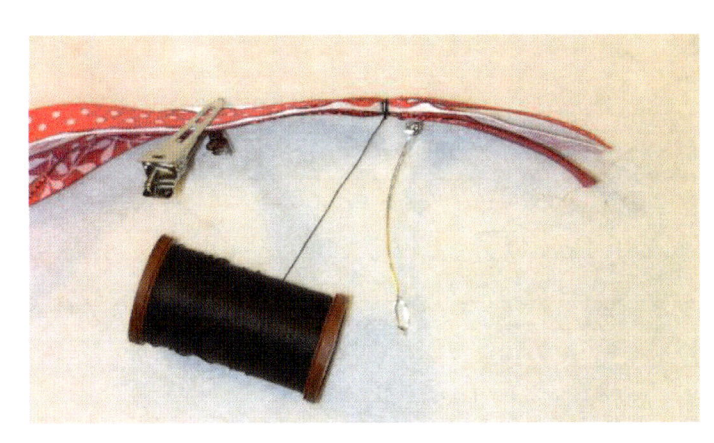

Using the thread, wrap the ribbon tightly around the edge of the barrette, as shown.

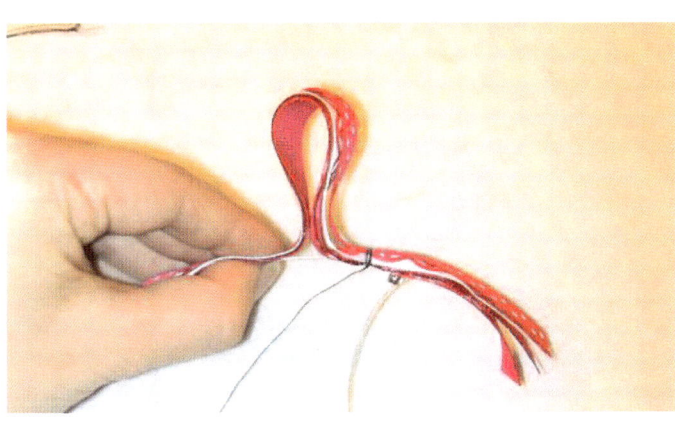

Loop the ribbon (the end closer to the roll) up. It can be as tall a loop as you'd like. I'd suggest 1.5-2" for a medium sized bow.

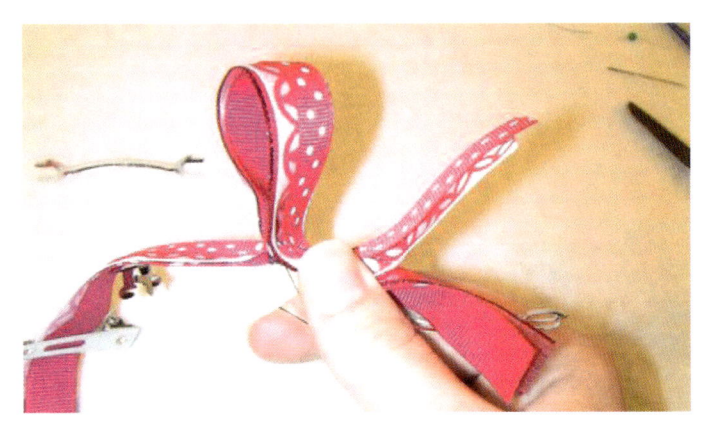

Now wrap the thread around the other side of the loop (the left side). Wrap it tightly 2-3 times. Continue to hold the thread securely so it doesn't unravel.

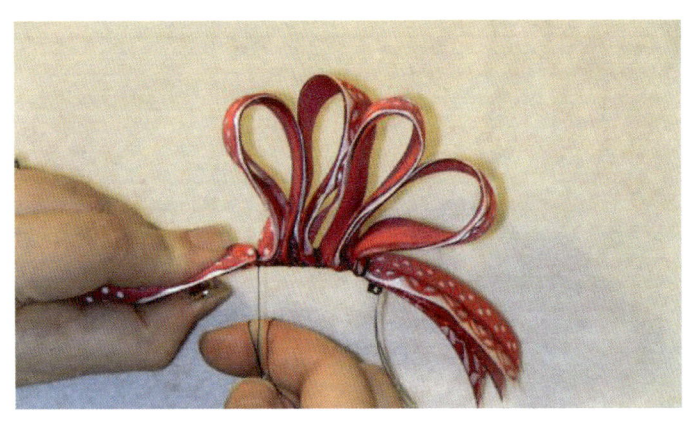

Continue to make loops (the same height) and wrap tightly as you go along. Do this until the barrette is full.
TIP: Slide the loops together and you'll have a much fuller bow.

Once you get to the end, wrap the thread tightly one final time and then knot it securely. You can now cut the thread off the roll.

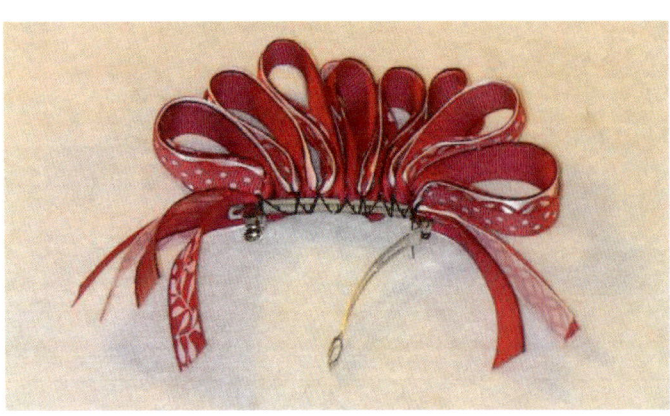

Here is what your bow looks like now. See the tails on each end? Those are about 2 inches long but you can make them as long as you'd like.

Copyright 2012.   LearnHowToMakeBows.com   LearnHowToMakeBows@gmail.com

Fluff out the loops on your bow in random order so they are nice and perky and full.

Don't forget to put the bottom piece back on the barrette!

Easy Bow

Supplies:
1.5" ribbon
Glue gun
Needle/thread
Scissors
Lighter

You'll need 2 pieces of ribbon that are twice the length of the bow you want to make. I'm using 8 inches for a 4 inch bow.

Loop the ribbon ends around and glue together. Do this with both pieces of ribbon so you have 2 circles formed.

Put a dab of glue in the center of the loop (on the "bad" side of the ribbon).

Pinch the loop together in the center.

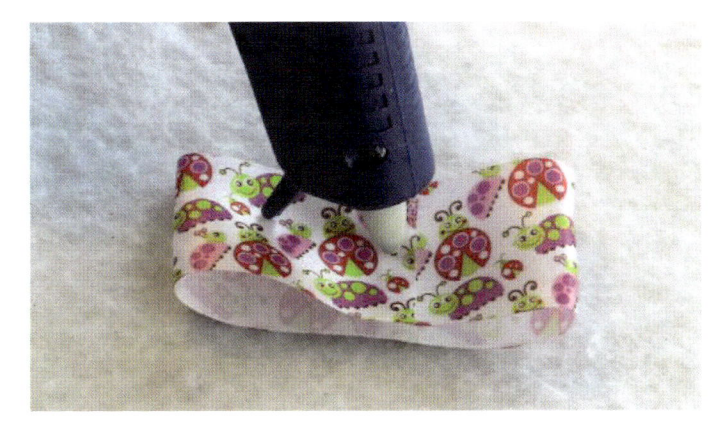

Place a dot of glue at the center. (I actually like to do this on the same side as the seam of the ribbon ends meeting.)

Fold the ribbon length-wise and hold for a second until the glue dries.

In the center of one side, place a dab of glue. (You'll do this step and the next one on the other side too!)

Fold the top ribbon down and hold in place. Be sure you just have that side of the ribbon being pulled down.

Now do these 2 steps on the other side of the ribbon.

Copyright 2012.   LearnHowToMakeBows.com   LearnHowToMakeBows@gmail.com

Here's what your bow looks like now. Make two of these.

Put the two bows together and be sure the creases at the center look nice. Pinch together tightly.

Wrap the center with thread or craft wire.

Cover the center of the bow with ribbon to hide the thread. Your bow is now ready to glue on to a lined clip.

Fun Sprays

Supplies:
Variety of ribbon widths (3/8" to 1.5")
Scissors
Lighter
Needle and thread
Hot glue

To start, cut three strips of 1.5" ribbon about 6 inches long.

Lay them on top of each other, spread out as shown.

Use a salon clip to hold in place then make 3 stitches directly up the center.

Remove the needle, pull the thread tightly and wrap around the center. Knot the thread at the back to secure in place.

To cut the edges in a triangle shape, fold the ribbon lengthwise as shown.

Cut on an angle, as shown.

While holding the ribbon ends together, heat seal it quickly with a lighter.

**Do NOT heat seal satin…it will burn!

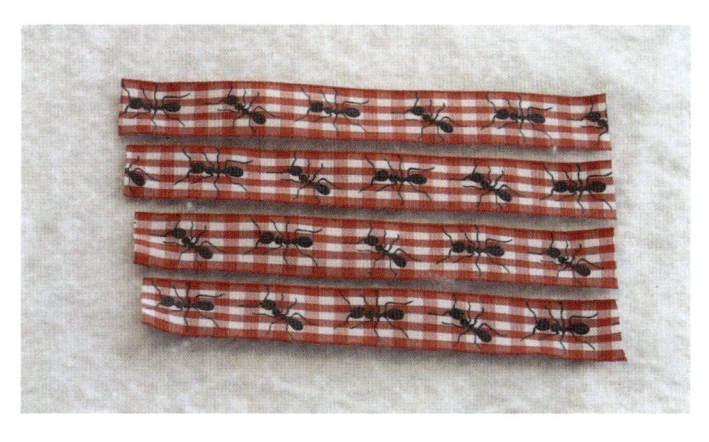

I'll show you this once more with 5/8" ribbon. I'm using 4 pieces that are 7 inches long. Here's a bit of a different way you can make these sprays.

Arrange the pieces around as shown. Trying to get them evenly spaced.

Bring a needle and thread up through the center of the sprays.

Now make 2-3 nice pinches across the center.

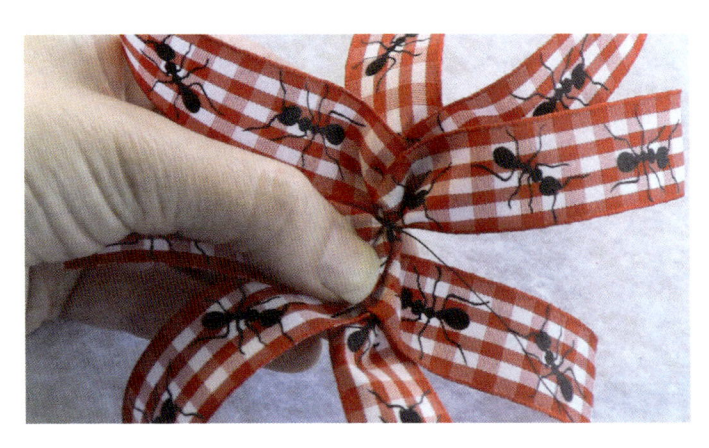

Wrap the thread tightly around the center, keeping your nice creases in place.

Copyright 2012.   LearnHowToMakeBows.com   LearnHowToMakeBows@gmail.com

Now bring the needle back and forth through the thread at the back to knot it tightly in place.

Here are the completed sprays.

Make as many as these as you want. I've created 4 layers of sprays for this bow.

Here are my four layers of sprays that are ready to be put together in a bow.

One at a time, glue down the layers together, in an order that looks nice to you.

Here's what I did (bottom to top): 1.5", 5/5", 3/8", 5/8"

Copyright 2012.   LearnHowToMakeBows.com   LearnHowToMakeBows@gmail.com

Here is the finished bow. You can wrap the center with thread and tie off at the back. This will help secure it in place. Then glue down on lined clip.

Twisted Boutique Bow with Sprays

Supplies:
2 types of 1.5" ribbon &2 types of 5/8" ribbon
Peel and Stick tape (Aleen's brand - double sided craft tape)
Salon clip
Scissors
Straight pin
Needle and thread
Piece of cardboard (mine is 6.5" wide)

Place the "bad" side of the two types of 1.5" ribbon together. We'll be working with the ribbon like this while keeping them on the rolls.

Hold the ribbon as shown on the cardbard and wrap it around the back side. The edge of the ribbon should be about ¼ to ½ inch from the edge of the cardboard.

Bring the end of the ribbon down the back side, then back up and around to the top again.

Wrap it one final time and you'll end with the ribbon at the top. Where my pointer finger is at the top is where I cut off the excess ribbon off the roll.

Copyright 2012.   LearnHowToMakeBows.com   LearnHowToMakeBows@gmail.com   57

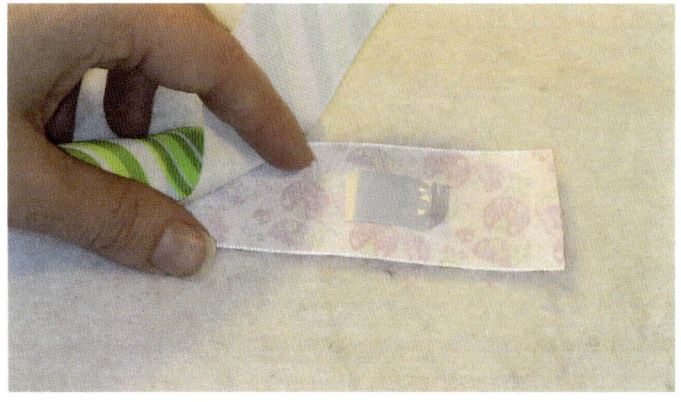

Remove the ribbon from the cardboard now. (That step was for us to measure out the ribbon length needed.) Secure your ribbons together in three places with a small piece of peel and stick tape.

Wrap the ribbon in the same manner you did earlier. Then place a straight pin directly through the center of the ribbon.

Gently remove the ribbon from the cardboard. Now we'll start separating the loops. The top ribbon tail goes to the right, the 1st loop at the top to the left, the 2nd loop at the top to the right.

Pull the loops out until you have a nice bow shaped form.

TIP: Pull loops from center, not from tips.

Copyright 2012.   LearnHowToMakeBows.com   LearnHowToMakeBows@gmail.com

Use a salon clip up the center to hold your bow in place. Be sure it is exactly centered. Make 3 stitches up the center.

Remove the clip and put the thread tightly. Be sure your peaks are forming nicely in the center as you pull.

Wrap the center with thread and knot at back.

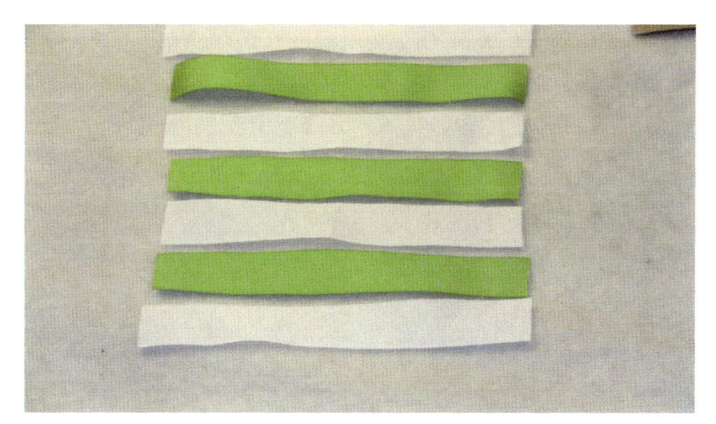

Now let's make the sprays with 6 pieces of 5/8" ribbon.

Spread out the ribbon pieces around in a circle, rotating the colors.

Make three stitches directly up the center. (There will be 6 ribbon ends on the right and 6 on the left.)

Pull the thread tightly then wrap the center a few times and tie a knot at the back. Your sprays are complete.

Now simple glue the bow you made on to the center of the sprays. Hot glue the bow on to a lined clip.

Layered Boutique Bow with Twister Top

Supplies:
2 colors of 1.5" ribbon
5/8" ribbon (for sprays)
3/8" ribbon (for center)
Needle and thread
Scissors
Lighter
Hot glue

Use the instructions of the previous bow to make a twisted boutique bow.

Now we need to find the length of ribbon for the sprays. My bow is 4 inches wide, so I'm going to cut my sprays ribbon at 7 inches to be sure I have plenty to work with.

Arrange your 4 pieces of ribbon around a circle, overlapping at the center.

Place a salon clip down the center to guide you. Make a few stitches up the center; I've made 4 here.

Copyright 2012.   LearnHowToMakeBows.com   LearnHowToMakeBows@gmail.com   62

Tightly pull the thread so nice peaks form across the center of your ribbons.

Wrap the thread around the center a few times then tie off at the back.

Glue the sprays down to the center of the basic boutique bow. As you can see they are plenty long enough so I can cut back later.

Now let's make the top twister bow. Layer your two 1.5" ribbons directly on top of each other and secure in a few places with peel and stick tape, if you'd like.

Copyright 2012.   LearnHowToMakeBows.com   LearnHowToMakeBows@gmail.com

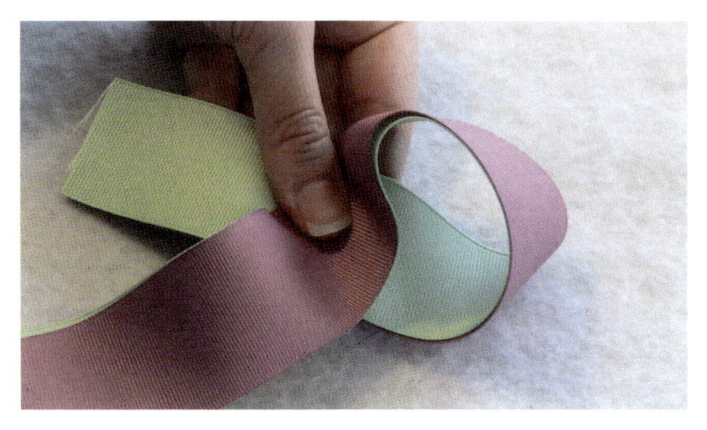

I like to work with the ribbon on the roll so I can move the ribbon around and get the perfect size to fit on top of my sprays. Loop the end around leaving a small tail.
(The green end is the tail.)

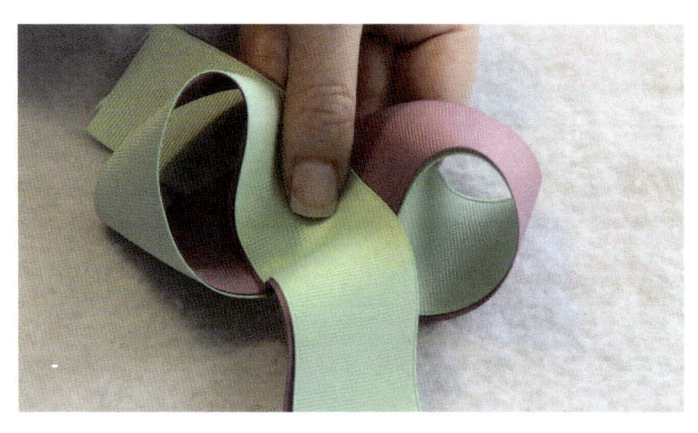

Bring the mauve end (from the previous photo) up and to the right to make a loop. Bring the tail down. The tails will be at the exact same angle to each other.

Place a salon clip up the center and make three stitches.

Pull the thread tightly and then wrap the center with thread. Tie off the thread at the back.

Copyright 2012.   LearnHowToMakeBows.com   LearnHowToMakeBows@gmail.com

Your twister bow is now complete.

Now we're ready to put together our bow. Cut your sprays however you prefer. I made mine a little longer than the base bow so they perk up a bit and look nice.

Finally, place the twister bow on top and wrap the center with the 3/8 inch thread. Hot glue on to a lined clip.

Surround a Bow

Supplies:
2 Twisted boutique bows (using 6.5 "and 4.5 " cardboard)
3/8" ribbon for loops
Scissors
Hot glue

Since you already know how to make the twisted boutique bow, we're going to start making the loops. Working on the roll we'll be looping the 3/8" ribbon around.

I like to pick up the bow the loops will surround (the top bow in this case) and place the 3/8" ribbon around one loop of the bow to get an idea of the size needed.

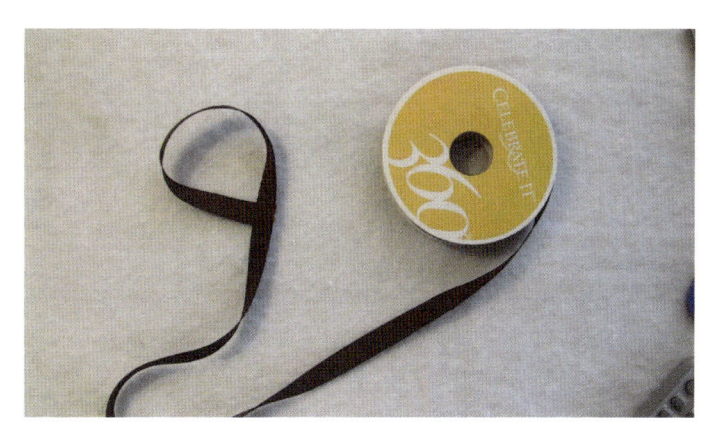

Once you have the exact size loop needed, glue the end of the ribbon down at a 90 degree angle.

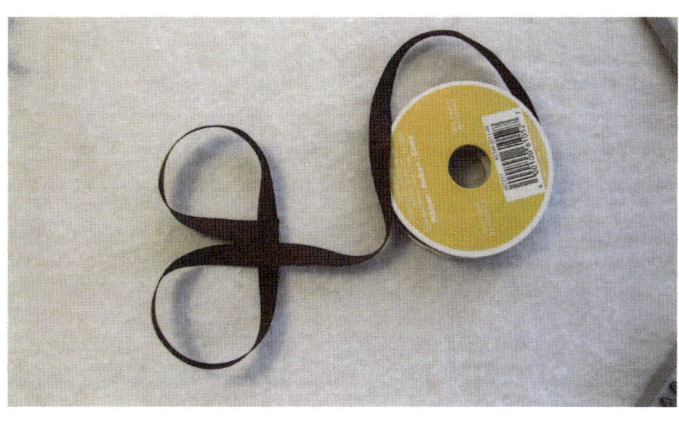

Now bring the ribbon up and around to form a second loop of the exact same size. Glue that down at the center.

Bring the ribbon down and around to make the third loop at the bottom right.

Make the fourth loop and glue at the center.

See how the ribbons are parallel as they meet in the center?

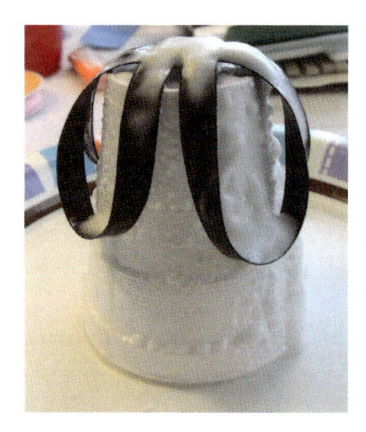

TIP: Place your loops upside down on a cup and spray well with Spray Starch (get in laundry aisle at grocery store). Allow to completely dry.

I love how perky this makes the loops!

Now we just need to assemble these 3 pieces by gluing the loops to the base bow, then the top bow on that. Finally, wrap a piece of 3/8" ribbon around the center to finish.

Layered Boutique Bow

Supplies:
2 colors of 1.5" ribbon (base bow and sprays)
2 colors of 3/8" ribbon (loops)
2 colors of 5/8" ribbon (top bow)
Needle and thread
Salon clip
Lighter
Scissors
Hot glue

Make a twisted boutique bow using a 6.5" template (this makes a 4 inch bow). Now measure out some ribbon for our loops. It's need to be 1.5 inches longer on each side (so 7 inches long).

Arrange 5 pieces of 1.5" ribbon around a circle as shown.

Make one stitch right in the center of the ribbon stack.

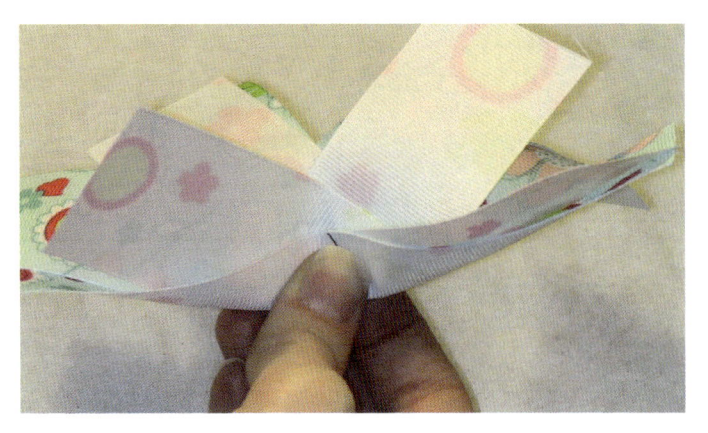

Carefully grab the ribbons and fold in half from bottom to top.

Now bring the edge of the ribbon back down to the bottom. Do this on both side. You've formed 2 nice peaks in the center of the bow.

Wrap the center with thread tightly, tie off at the back.

Cut the ends however you prefer.

Now you can hot glue those sprays right on to the center of the base twisted bow. I like to actually flip the twisted boutique bow upside down so the bottom is facing up!

Now make another 2 layered twisted boutique bow with the 4 inch wide template. Grab your 3/8" ribbon and make a loop behind the bow to get the size.

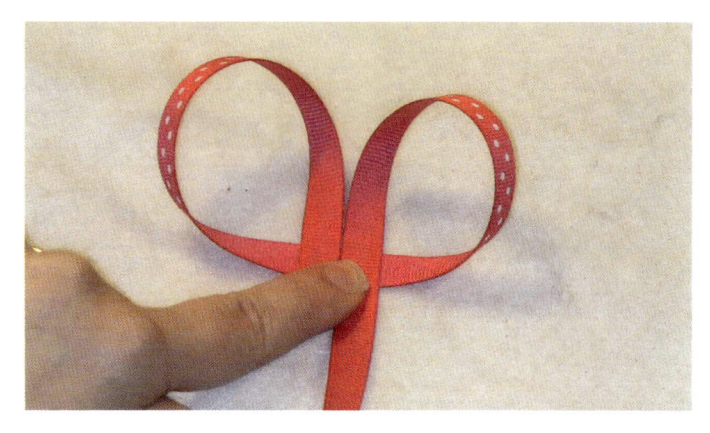

Continue making loops (as shown on previous bow) until you have 4 loops exactly the same size formed.

To make the second layer of loops we'll use a second color ribbon. With the light pink ribbon you will follow the previously made loops around and glue them down just a bit smaller than the dark pink loops.

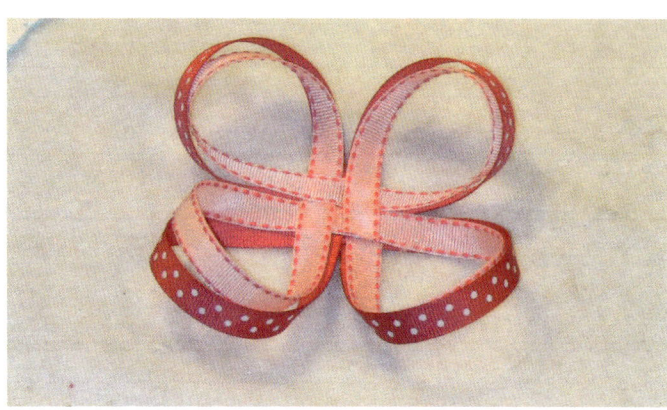

Here is the completed set of double loops.

Now assemble the bow by adding the loops on top of the sprays you already glued down. Finally place the smaller twisted boutique bow on top.

Copyright 2012.   LearnHowToMakeBows.com   LearnHowToMakeBows@gmail.com

Helpful Tips for Beginner Bow Makers

Always heat seal the ends of your grosgrain ribbon with the quick pass of a lighter. Do not use a lighter on satin ribbon as it will burn. You could also purchase "Fray Check" at a craft store and use that to seal your ends.

Be sure to center the stitches up the middle of your bow exactly even so you'll have a perfect finished bow.

Check the sizes of the loops of your bows to be sure they are the same size before wrapping the center of your bow.

Use a piece of cardboard with a slit up the center (just a few inches) in order to make twisted boutique bows easy!

Experiment with all the different types of bows you know how to make. Layer bows, sprays, and loops to form lots of beautiful layered boutique bows.

If you're not sure how big you want to make your bow, work with the ribbon on the roll and play around with it before you make a cut.

*** Watch the DVD when it arrives, since you'll get extra tips and very detailed step-by-step directions as I walk you through each bow in this manual. ***

Email me if you still have questions:
LearnHowToMakeBows@gmail.com

Happy Bow Making!
Jenn
LearnHowToMakeBows.com

FAQs

Have a question about learning how to make hair bows? Send me an email (**learnhowtomakebows@gmail.com**) and I'll answer your email. No question is too small!

Question: What can i use to get the excess glue off without ruining the ribbon that it's on?

Answer: To remove excess hot glue you can carefully warm it up near a lighter (not close enough to burn the ribbon!) or place it in the freezer for an hour or so then the hot glue typically will be able to be cracked off.

Question: I am new at making the bows and I thought about making bows to go on little girls flip flops. Was wondering what was the best way to attach the bows. Hot glue them? I don't think using a clip would work, but really didn't know. Could you help me with this? thanks so much

Answer: Hi there, I would hot glue them and even secure them around the flip flop with a center piece of ribbon to stay in place. Hope that helps! I wouldn't use a clip only because I don't think it would be too comfortable to wear.

Question: What do I do to make the bows hold their shape? Some of the ribbon I use stays flimsy when I finish the bow what can I do to correct that?

Answer: I like to spray them down really well with starch and then blow dry them upside down with a hair dryer on a warm setting. This will help to keep it stiff and in place. I like the starch the best because it is really inexpensive, but you could also spray the finished bow with hairspray like AquaNet. Note: If you want to spray korker ribbon, it needs to be done while the ribbon is still rolled around the dowel and must dry completely before removing from the dowel (or else it will come un-korked VERY easily!)

Question: What are the three best bows for beginners to make?

Answer: I would suggest learning the twisted boutique bow. It's not the easiest but it is part of a lot of layered boutique bows so it's great to know how to make it. It takes some practice to get the loops down correctly. After that I'd say two easy and FUN ones would be loopy bows and korker bows.

Question: I was wondering what is the best size ribbon to make korkers from?

Answer: Definitely 1/4 inch or 3/8 inch is best because the ribbon stays korked the best. Also, grosgrain ribbon should always be used. Satin ribbon is really difficult to use for korkers since they come undone very easily.

Question: I was wondering what clip is best to use on different bows? Are certain ones better for different types of bows, or is it just personal preference?

Answer: It really is a personal preference the majority of the time. With one exception….for loopy bows it is very challenging to make that on an alligator clip, so I always use a French barrette. Otherwise I put all my bows on lined alligator clips. You can certainly use French barrettes on any of them if you prefer though.

Question: I've loved your courses. I have gotten real "specific" and make primarily loopy bows. What are the BEST ribbons (material-wise) for loopy bows…so they stand up well and aren't too flimsy during the creation part? Thanks!

Answer: I've found that using a variety of ribbons really helps. I prefer grosgrain and never make my loops more than 2 inches tall. Having at least the majority of your ribbons as grosgrain will definitely help with the creation part and if you have one or two with print on them, they tend to be sturdier ribbon to work with since the print often adds some weight and stiffness to the ribbon. The taller you make the loops, the floppier they will be. Also, have you tried starching them one the bow is made? I'd spray it really well with starch and then hold it upside down and dry it gently with a hairdryer. That will really help to make the loops stay perky!

Made in the USA
Lexington, KY
20 December 2012